M. (Michael) Wineburgh

Where to Spend the Winter Months

A Birdseye View of a Trip to Mexico, Via Havana

M. (Michael) Wineburgh

Where to Spend the Winter Months
A Birdseye View of a Trip to Mexico, Via Havana

ISBN/EAN: 9783337145248

Printed in Europe, USA, Canada, Australia, Japan

Cover: Foto ©Andreas Hilbeck / pixelio.de

More available books at **www.hansebooks.com**

WHERE TO SPEND THE

WINTER MONTHS.

———•———

A BIRDSEYE VIEW

OF A TRIP TO

MEXICO,

VIA HAVANA.

———•••———

,BY

M. WINEBURGH.

NEW YORK:

M. WINEBURGH & CO., 55 & 57 BEAVER STREET

1880.

PRELUDE.

We take pleasure in offering these lines to the traveling world. They embrace useful instructions in relation to the most agreeable and economical method of traveling between New York and Mexico, via Havana.

The late visit of the Chicago merchants and also that of General Grant, has caused a greater interest among Americans in that country. The discovery of several very rich mines and the renewed efforts of railroad schemes have directed much attention to our sister Republic. For the past few years a large number of Americans have visited the city of Mexico, and it is probable that every year will bring that sunny land of plenty into greater favor with tourists and pleasure seekers. But to the ordinary American, Mexico is a *terra incognito*. Every one has some misty recollections of Montezuma and Cortez, of Iturbide and Maximilian; of wonderful prehistoric ruins and Eldorados hidden by a conquered race. But unfortunately the difficulties and modes of travel are unknown to the average tourist, and the means of finding out the necessary information, which has not until now been published, has caused many sightseers to abandon a delightful trip. The uncertainty that prevails in regard to the government and the supposed want of adequate protection have prevented the tourist from visiting a country which may truly be termed the promised land of American commerce. The information which we intend to give our reader about its climate and productions may not be uninteresting even to those who may never visit Mexico.

An extended experience as a merchant and traveler, and a carefully written *note-book*, form the material from which this work is compiled.

To travel with comfort and security, a knowledge of the country we contemplate visiting, as well as the customs and peculiarities of its inhabitants, will be esteemed as valuable.

Practical experience is our guide; we offer it to our readers; we will point out the places of interest and indicate the best manner to reach them. We will in short lead our traveler safely around the many reefs, with which inexperience so frequently comes in contact.

M. WINEBURGH.

BEFORE WE START.

If you are going to Cuba procure your passport. This document you will obtain in the following manner: Make affidavit before a notary public as regards your nationality and description of person, forward it to the State Department at Washington, and they will send you one.

The passport may include more than one person, members of the same family, and is necessary before the passage ticket is issued.

The passport will be vised by the Spanish consul 29 Nassau street, his fees are $2.00 gold for this service. Upon boarding the vessel you will hand it, together with the passage ticket to the *purser* who will deliver them to the boarding officer upon reaching Havana; the boarding officer will return it to you when you land; if you are in transit for Mexico no passport is required. For tourists the most agreeable and pleasant route between New York, Havana and Mexico is that offered by the steamers of Messrs. F. Alexandre & Sons. This company offers superior accommodations and increased facilities at more reasonable rates than any other line running to Cuba or Mexico; it is the only line which goes direct to Mexico. The accommodations on this line of steamers are unsurpassed. The Messrs. F. Alexandre & Sons are proverbial for their untiring efforts to give their patrons the greatest amount of pleasure and comfort at the most reasonable rates ; the appointments of all their steamers are of the best order, the captains and officers are experienced seamen and pay particular attention to the comfort and pleasure of their passengers ; the steamers of this line were all built especially for the trade in which they are engaged.

Now let us refer to the baggage : besides your trunks, take along a valise or two, in which place such articles of wearing apparel as you may need during the passage (your trunks will be accessible only during certain hours of the morning;) trunks, unless of small size, are not allowed in the state room, and for comfort it is better not to have them.

As you are going to the Antilles, a very warm climate, it will not be necessary to intimate that furs and heavy clothing may be dispensed with.

The most convenient manner of arranging your cash account, is to invest your funds in letters of credit (procurable at our banking houses) reserving sufficient to defray your immediate expenses until you reach your first correspondent or banker in Havana or Vera Cruz as the case may be.

Letters of introduction are always desirable, and should be procured if possible. When we land in an entirely strange place, and are unacquainted with its language and customs we are, so to speak, excommunicated from its society. A letter of introduction is of material service. The Spanish race, as a rule, are hospitable and kind-hearted. They will always receive you with open arms when you introduce yourself as a medium of mutual acquaintance and friendship.

LEAVING THE PORT OF NEW YORK.

If the steamer starts at 3 o'clock P. M. be sure to be on board at 2 P. M.; give your baggage in charge of the porter of the vessel, take your valises to your state room, then you may quietly adjourn to the deck, and indulge in a segar while viewing the hurried parting scene in which so many excited people figure. Do not forget to fee the steward who shows you to your state room, he will remember the attention and you will invest a dollar at profitable interest, payable in good services during the trip.

There is nothing so conducive to comfort as *keeping cool.* A hurried man traveling invariably forgets important duties while attending to matters of comparative insignificance.

THE START.

The time for departure has arrived at last; a shrill whistle announces the fact that all those who are not to sail, must retire to the dock, where they may wave their last adieus to those leaving the port.

This scene is one of confusion to say the least. Here we have a second Babel wherein the confusion of tongues, to say nothing of lips, is conspicuously boisterous. The gang plank creaks its displeasure at being burdened in so unceremonious a manner; it threatens to give way and drop the excited multitude into a briny bath below. Good bye! take care of yourself, write soon! where's my poodle? Oh! that dog will be left! my trunk will not reach here in time. O! my! what shall I do. Ah! here it comes, thank—&c. In the distance we observe an express wagon and a lame horse whose one weather eye is trying to pick out one of Mr. Bergh's agents in that motley crowd.

You, reader, are all right, because you came on board in good time and have nothing more to do, but to look on. Have you seen the life saving apparatus? Do so, in case of accident it is well to know where to look for help. There should be at least two life preservers in your stateroom; see that you are supplied in this particular. Upon the door you will find instructions regarding the particular life boat assigned to you in case of accident, take a look at the boat.

At last the gang plank is removed. How many persons remain on shore! There are sad faces too, and moistened eyes, Miss ―――― has two diamonds trembling upon her dark eyelashes and a young fellow on board is making vain efforts to look pleasantly at her.

Handkerchiefs wave a last adieu, and tears render more dim the progressive distance which goes on widening between regrets, hopes and fears. Off she goes down the bay upon her majestic career toward the sunny South, new scenes and novel experiences.

AT SEA.

Here we are, gliding upon the broad and undulating bosom of the Atlantic about 1200 miles from Havana which we will reach in from 4 to 4½ days.

Is this your first experience at sea? In that case you will be struck with the immensity of space that lies before you. Cast your eyes in whatever direction you may, water—water—water—and sky—sky meet your gaze. Keep on deck as much as possible and avoid thinking of being sick. In the early morn one rises and appears on deck; the first carress of an amorous sun spreads its brilliant rays upon the waters of the deep.

Our gallant craft maintains her 16 knots an hour with the regularity of a well regulated chronometer. A distant horizon separates us now from home, another one invites us to look beyond its line, and as we proceed onward the same invitation is repeated indefinitely. We are thus flowing along at the dawn of day.

A gentle breeze ruffles the crystal surface. As we proceed toward our journey's end we leave in our wake an effervescent foam which melts away in the course of time as do remembrances. Far in the distance a sail is seen and now and then a school of porpoises lend a singular movement and life in contrast with the calm surface of the ocean.

After steaming for 25 hours we are in the latitude of Cape Hatteras; rough weather often prevails in this quarter, although we have passed the Cape without experiencing unusual winds or seas, nor their attending discomforts and fears.

IN SIGHT OF LAND.

On the third day of our journey, the coast of Florida appears in the distance on our right ; it suggests, most agreeably, that in case of danger *terra firma* is within our reach. Men naturally prefer to take risks in a familiar atmosphere; land to man is what water is to the population of the briny deep. All day the Florida coast remains in perspective, and the scene viewed from beneath our awnings is exceedingly interesting, especially so to the novice traveler. One does not become tired of this panoramic view. Reclining upon a comfortable camp chair and enjoying a good cigar, we watch the distant shores which recede as we pass them, to make room for new and interesting landscapes which appear in the horizon unceasingly, until the veil of twilight and the evening mist suggests the approach of night to close the last act of our third day's sail.

The next morning our noble craft enters the port of Havana, one of the finest harbors in the world. A fleet of small boats immediately surround us and dance merrily upon the white capped waves, as though they were pleased to welcome our majestic presence. These boats are to the Bay of Havana what the hacks are to that city, with this difference, that the boats solicit our patronage, while the hack drivers remain sound asleep upon their boxes and await our orders.

These little boats transport us and our baggage to the shore for a small pecuniary consideration. They are not however admitted to board our distinguished decks until the formalities of the law have been attended to. The custom house officials and the Board of Health have a prior claim to our attention. After the official duties have been performed, the occupants of the small boats are allowed to present to us their respects, which ceremony they perform in a somewhat eccentric manner. Most of these individuals have some Cuban interest to represent; some are hotel agents, each of which claims to offer extraordinary advantages over the attributes of a neighbor. The Hotel San Carlos or Hotel Pasagé are first class houses, and we can also recommend the Hotel Ingletera and Hotel Telegrafo as respectable resorts which are frequented by Americans; the board is $2.50 to $5.00 gold by the day, or $1½ gold for room and meals à la carte.

If you intend to return to the vessel to continue your voyage to Mexico, you need only take with you a valise, which hand to the hotel agent whom you have agreed to accompany. Leave all the details of your baggage and tickets to the charge of your hotel guide. We have always found it profitable to fee these men, as it secures to us their best attention. If you have any baggage they will pass it without trouble or delay. Tourists in transit may remain on board the steamer, there is no extra charge.

Now we climb down the sides of our steamer and enter the diminutive craft which in point of size, when compared to our Ocean Queen, appears as a mere nut shell. These small boats are however perfectly safe, being built for rough weather and high winds; they have great breadth of beam and stand up firmly to any wind, in fact it may be said that it is almost impossible to cap-size them.

Once embarked in our little transport, we launch off for the wharf and move along at a very fair rate of speed. There is a canvas roof over us which affords a welcome shade against the rays of a powerful sun. We are going to the custom house dock, to go through an official examination in relation to our baggage; this formality does not occupy much time, and we are very soon relieved by the refreshing information on the part of the officers that *it is all right*, no duty to pay as we have with us only such articles as we need for our personal comfort. The custom house officers as a rule are both obliging and civil, which is not a little acceptable to strangers in a foreign land. They examine carefully for all kinds of literature

We pass the custom house gates and are practically free to act. Here we are in Havana; an attractive scene presents itself to our every inquiry. Houses of variegated colors and rank vegetation predominate.

We require a hack; one is at hand, the coachman asleep upon his box, our guide wakes his independent lethargy by means of a poke with a parasol, and the driver is at our service for the small sum of 40 cents paper (equal to 18 cents of our money). He obligingly offers to drive us to Kamtschatka, but we merely accept his good offices as far as the hotel, where he drives us, bag and baggage, all without extra charge.

It must be observed here that to experience real comfort we should follow the customs of the localities we visit. Cubans move about quietly and remain cool ; let us imitate their example, for the rapid movements of a New Yorker is poorly adapted to the temperature and habits of Havana. It may be difficult at first to accustom ourselves to the ways which tropical climates demand, but necessity will soon compel us to follow the example of the indigenous population.

Havana is built upon a tongue of land, the head of which is braced and defended by the heights of Cabanas and the Moro Castle. As usual in all old cities the most ancient portion is invariably constructed in old fashioned style, narrow streets and small dwellings form a contrast with the more recently developed districts. In the *Old Havana* (so to speak) dwellings, shops, warehouses and churches are cramped up in confusion, whereas in the modern quarters of the city, the architecture and plans of streets and avenues are in conformity with the world's most progressive ideas. The dwellings as a rule are only two stories high, but these have ceilings 20 feet from the floors, making the height of the houses 40 feet or equal to our three story houses in New York. All nationalities are found in harmonious association, and each conforming to the laws which nature suggests for the sake of comfort and health under a tropical sun. Many of the principal streets of Havana have awnings stretched across them.

A section of the city is abandoned to the Coolies or Chinese slaves; they having served a certain term of bondage in the service of some Cuban plantation, retire to that part of the city, to finish, with the least possible hardship, a life which they commenced under the trying auspices of a semi-barbarous regime.

Havana occupies a territory of about five square leagues or fifteen square miles. Its population will reach 250,000.

In times gone by the city was encircled by massive walls and deep trenches, such as formed the defenses of the ancient European cities. But recently all this has been done away with, and Havana has assumed to a considerable degree the garb, fashions and manners of the age.

On either side of the Paseo (an avenue almost comparable to the Avenue des Champs Elysées of Paris) we observe handsome dwellings and delightful gardens; a profusion of flowers and immense palm trees form a grateful shade and spread their perfume through the atmosphere. This avenue is frequented by the *beau monde* of Havana. Thousands of vehicles convey the human flowers of female propriety to places of amusement or upon social visits. The brilliant colors, laces, silks and diamonds contrast charmingly with the more substantial physical beauty of the fair *donas*.

A WORD ABOUT CUBA.

Cuba lies between the latitude from about the twentieth degree north to the twenty-third, and between the seventy-fourth and eighty-fifth degree of west longitude. Its greatest length is 760 miles and its width varies from 20 to 135 miles. It embraces 47,278 square miles. (New York State has 47,000 square miles.)

The entire coast line of Cuba is 2,220 miles and is generally dangerous to shipping, yet the island possesses over two hundred ports including sheltered landings. A range of mountains run its entire length and contain the head waters of many streams that flow north and south into the Gulf and the Ca ribbean Sea.

The climate is warm and dry during the greater part of the year, but it is more temperate than other countries of the same latitude. The thermometer never rises as high as it does in New York.

In Cuba are found almost all the important minerals. There are two seasons, the rainy and the dry; the former begins in May and lasts till November. The products are tobacco, sugar, fruits and hardwoods. The vegetation is rich.

The inhabitants are mostly of Spanish and African descent. The children of foreigners born in Cuba and the Southern countries are called Creoles. Towards these the Spaniards experience a positive dislike, and that feeling is fully reciprocated by the Creoles. In 1862 the population of Cuba was 1,359,438. A law passed in June 23, 1873, declared all slaves free, but the Government has never been able to enforce it. Besides Havana, which has 250,000 inhabitants, there are thirteen other cities, twelve towns and 324 villages and hamlets. The productive industry is mainly devoted to the cultivation of sugar and tobacco. Cotton is also cultivated, but not extensively. Large crops of the silkworm are yearly raised. Cuba is subject to Spain and is governed absolutely by a Captain General.

A cigar and comfortable chair in *al fresco* with the news of the day affords a pleasant pastime during the torrid hours. If you can have a letter of introduction to a resident in Havana you may call upon him after dinner; you will find him frank, hospitable and polite. The customs in Cuba are very different from those observed in the United States in this respect. In Cuba *the houses are as open as the hearts*, and you are welcome to both. Discreet people will not abuse this Southern hospitality, and will consequently retain the good graces of their generous hosts.

One of the principal as well as one of the most agreeable and brilliant displays to be witnessed by the tourist is the plaza of Havana on a fine evening. Here he can behold the life of the city in all its beauty and gaiety amidst thousands of gas jets, which seems to defy the sun in brightness, and hear delicious strains of music discoursed by a' fine military band. Among the numerous and splendid Cafés which line all sides the plaza youth, beauty, aristocracy, and fashion come to spend the evening to partake of a cup of coffee or to sip some of the many cooling drinks of which there are plenty and of many kinds. The Cubans are very courteous to strangers and it is much safer to stroll among the crowds then it would be under similar circumstances in New York. A visit to any of the numerous Cigar and Cigarette manufacturers will be found very interesting.

LIFE IN CUBA.

There is still another peculiarity observable in Cuba, not less striking than the dressing of the children. The merchant or storekeeper does not designate his place of business by putting his name on a sign over the door or anywhere on the house; nor does he show by any word or mark that he has anything for sale, but it seems he acts or does business on the principle that if anybody wants to know where he resides, or what kind of goods he has to sell, it is the buyer's and not the seller's business to find out the best way he can, when and where such goods are to be had. When I say *when*, I mean that if you, after some difficulty, at last find his store, and get there between 11 and 12 o'clock, you may find the whole business *personnel* at breakfast, and have to wait until they return. From this you may conclude that the merchant in Havana takes it easy. Others again, maintain that their house is so old that everybody knows or ought to know, where they hold forth, and what kind of goods they keep, without thinking that the world moves on, that every day new men spring up, or strangers want to find their place of business. But as this unreasonable conservatism and exclusiveness is practiced by all old and well established business houses, they are very proud of it. It is extensively imitated by young and newly established firms, because they, too, want to be considered old and above the necessity of telling the public who and what they are; and if a long established merchant should venture the innovation to put his name over his door it would be considered that there was something out of order in the premises. It is only the retailers and other small traders who condescend to show their names in connection with their business. Others adopt some fancy title or the name of some prominent saint to designate their establishment, such as The Golden Eagle, the Española, Santa Catalina, &c., the same as we in America adopt a trade mark. Anything is considered better than their name, which they anxiously and studiously try to conceal. That there is but little advertising in newspapers, where the names are shown with so much reluctance, is self-evident.

So things go on in the old rut from one generation to another, and no effort is made to follow the laudable example of other countries. It seems the Spanish character is quite self-sufficient and will not bend to be taught by others, and will not admit a possibility of error. The people are very closely wedded to their national prejudices; in fact, Cuba at this moment is probably the most old-fashioned country in the world, and it is only when pressed upon by absolute necessity that she reluctantly admits an innovation.

As we pass along in our Victoria (many of these vehicles are used here), we have a very general view, not only of the many fine residences but also of the inmates thereof. It is customary to sit near the large apertures which in New York might be known as windows; glass is not used in these windows and a necessity for closing them never occurs in this climate.

Smoking is not objected to by the fair sex, some of whom not infrequently indulge in a cigarette. The ladies are not given to walking, they seldom venture out except in a carriage. The *Quitrin* or Victoria is the popular conveyance in Havana. The fair ones do their shopping in these, and the poor clerks and salesmen are compelled to bring their wares to the Victoria for their inspection, from which one may easily estimate the activity of the former and the good nature of the latter who knows no limit to his complaisance. Would it not be a little amusing to witness the same amount of condescension on the part of A. T. Stewart's clerks? And what confusion would it not give.

The Roman Catholic religion prevails almost exclusively; in this particular the women are, as in this country, *the pillars* of the church; there are no pews in the Havana churches, the congregation being obliged either to bring chairs with them or remain standing or kneeling during the ceremony ; a small cushion is usually brought with the chair. The manner in which Sunday is observed (we should say enjoyed), because the Spaniards and French and other enlightened people consider it a day of rest from the toils of the week, and take the liberty of interpreting rest as they please and not as the Puritans chose to prescribe. In consequence of this the Sunday in Havana (as it is in Paris) is devoted to amusements and a pleasant relaxation from the arduous strain of the week of labor.

The theatres, among which we find the great *Tacon*, the *La Paz Opera House* and the American Circus are all open on Sundays, as well as the *Louvre Café*. The *Casino Español*—a political club of national influence is the *rendez-vous* of the most distinguished men of Havana. Every one has heard of the celebrated bull fights of Cuba; this amusement is of ancient and national origin. These fights are held outside of the city limits every Sunday. Horse cars run to within a few blocks of the place which is named Plaza de Torros. We regret to say that these fights do not strike us as conducive to either refinement or enlightenment; it savors of barbarism and those animal instincts which form the larger half of human nature under all social regimes.

At some of the leading hotels, such as the Hotel Pasage and the Hotel Inglaterra, Protestant religious services are held for the accommodation of transient guests.

The Cubans with the enthusiasm of their Latin neighbors of Europe, celebrate the great Carnival which precedes Lent. Immense processions of masqueraders parade the streets and avenues and form a human kaleidoscope of indefinite lights, shades and colors. The entire population appears to be wrapped in the pleasure of making a fool of itself, and he is a fool who will not follow the people in this whirlwind of folly and fun.

The Cuban character is a combination of pride, chivalry, indolence, love, hospitality and jealousy. Look out for the *old husband* of a young wife, be careful not to be too demonstrative in your administration of his better and more attractive half, for he is as jealous of her as it is possible to be. The women in this respect not infrequently commit an involuntary murder by encouraging the attentions of young admirers, drawing them closer and closer to the dangerous reefs, as did the siren of mythological celebrity.

The music in Havana is good and as greatly appreciated as it is in the United States. During the winter months an excellent Italian Opera Troupe is handsomely supported.

The suburbs of Havana are really charming, composed in great part of picturesque country residences where good taste is united to comfort and health. A favorite ground for pic-nics is Puentes Grandes (Big Bridge); here among other attractions is a fine beach for bathing, and a few miles up the coast are famous fishing grounds. To the eastward the town of Guanabaca is much frequented as a summer resort and is noted for its mineral springs. A few miles to the west the traveler will be interested in visiting an ancient and mysterious castle, the dingy architecture of which reminds us of the feudal ages and of knight errants of old.

The waters of the Bay bathe the foundations of this antique relic of the past; visitors may reach this old curiosity by taking the steam cars which pass out of the *Avenue del Norte.*

Among the attractions which are most interesting to the merchant is the wharves which are not as extensive as the trade of Havana appears to demand; in fact most of the loading and unloading is done by means of *lighters.*

The wharves consist of a mile or so of roofed levees to which are moored vessels, their bows facing the shore and packed like sardines side by side.

MATANZAS.

The second city in importance is reached by rail in a few hours; it lies in the valley of Yamuri, has a population of 40,000 and in most respects resembles Havana. Good hotels are found in this place. Among the attractions the scenery is esteemed as most remarkable for its romantic beauty. The Caves of Bellamar and the valley of Yumiri are visited by many tourists; it takes two hours by the Havana Bay and Matanzas railroad which leaves Havana almost every hour.

The next place of importance is Cardenas, situated on the Northern coast; here we find an extensive sugar trade, doing a business of many millions a year; which is exported to the United States.

Cienfuegos may be visited with interest. This city lies upon the Iouthern coast, has a fine land-locked harbor, and is an important factor in the Cuban trade; here English is very generally spoken. There are steamers from this port to Batabano and recently railroad communications have been made direct to Havana, running through the sugar districts. There are also steamers from Cienfuegos to Santiago de Cuba on the Eastern end of the Island.

Not far from Cienfuegos is the ancient town of Trinidad, a place well worth visiting on account of its scenery.

We would also recommend a trip to Santiago de Cuba. This town does an extensive export trade in tobacco, sugar and coffee and is noted for its extensive copper mines; we meet in this place many French people. Santiago de Cuba was formerly the capital of Cuba; it is probably the most ancient town in the West Indies. Steamers from the United States and Europe touch at this port.

Those desiring to visit the places to which we have briefly alluded, can do so in the space of a month, and returning to Havana will find a transport for *Mexico waiting for them. If the visit is confined to the city of Havana the traveler's trunks remain in the hold of the steamer, which stays in port two days, after which she continues her journey to Progreso.

Once more we jump in a harbor boat and steer for the gallant craft which is getting up steam preparatory to an early start; many a warm shake of the hand intimates to us that we leave kind friends in Havana, and our experiences in that city are to be remembered with pleasure. We may not have escaped the captivating glance of a *dona;* perchance there may have been an interchange of sentiments which hold our affections more firmly than we would like to admit. At all events our visit to Havana has not passed without interest.

ON TO PROGRESO.

And now we plow the mighty deep, again resuming our journey to the Aztec capital.

We will not pretend to describe the country we are about to visit except in a general manner; volumes can be written upon this topic. The limited space to which our Guide is confined, restricts our observations to mere outlines. Our traveler's experience as he proceeds will complete our rough sketches, we are convinced, to his or her entire satisfaction. Being already familiar with *life at sea* we will not recapitulate its varied phases.

We reach Progreso after two days journey in the gulf. Progreso is the seaport of the city of Merida, the steamer remains there about tweny-four hours, thus enabling the tourist to land and visit the City of Merida, twenty-two miles distant—a railroad recently built connects Progreso with Merida—the capital of Yucatan; the fare is only a few dollars, and the trip will be found full of interest. Merida is a beautiful and quaint old city of 50,000 inhabitants, and is reached in about a half hours ride. The market place, which occupies an immense square, is situated about two blocks from the Hotel and about the same direction from the plaza, it is surrounded by a high adobe wall which is plastered on the sides fronting the streets. I entered the wide gate and was instantly surrounded by a crowd of Indian market women who pushed their wares almost in my face, and implored me in the name of the Blessed Virgin to patronize them. Their articles of sale were many and of various kinds: one old octogenarian Indian squaw wanted me to buy a coarse cotton chemise, which, she assured me, was well sewn, another a very pretty mestiza urged me to buy a small gourd rattle or children.

A very pleasant hour can be spent wandering through the market place; the streets of Merida are named from animals and birds, as the Indian population of the city is by no means a learned one, and as so few of them know how to read, the figures of the animals stand prominently on street corners to show the inquiring what street they may be walking on. Near the city of Valladolid in the eastern portion of the Peninsula of Yucatan there are about forty different ancient towns and cities in ruins, they have all been studied at one time or another by scientific men, who have not as yet come to any agreement as to their origin. The ruins consist principally of immense buildings which must have been used as palaces, temples, and castles, and buried beneath them are supposed to be images and other objects which decorated the buildings when the race of people, who built them were in existence. There have been many prominent Americans who have visited these ruins, and there have been, we believe, a few books written on the subject, the people who reside in and about the ruined cities have no legend of their origin. The antiquarian who wishes to visit them for purposes of study or curiosity will be amply compensated for his trouble. We understand that there are some ingenious Yankees, who are building a road from Merida to connect with these ruins, and in a short time we may hear of a better conveyance to these interesting cities than now exist; after leaving Progreso, Campeche and Frontera are the intermediate ports at which we stop on our way to Vera Cruz.

In Sight of Land.

The snow capped summit of the extinct volcano at Orizaba appears before us, and yet we are 60 miles from sight of the coast. This majestic apparition seems to form a part of the heavens, its hoary locks suggest almost an antediluvian origin; as we approach, it appears to rise higher and higher in the clouds in a truly imperial manner, and one cannot refrain from being deeply impressed with the comparative insignificance of its surroundings.

Four hours more and we perceive in the distant horizon the first outlines of the Vera Cruz coast. Soon we will be in port; the passengers appear well pleased. The last moments of a journey are always attended with pleasure. Those who have been sick are promptly convalescent and those who have enjoyed the trip are also well pleased to change the life at sea for one in which the pleasant anticipations of new scenes and strange enjoyments invite bright speculation. Curiosity is one of man's most salient characteristics and a change of scene is food for inquiry.

STREET SCENE IN VERA CRUZ.

The port of Vera Cruz is now distinctly seen. Coral reefs extend in a parallel line with the coast directly in front of the city, so that we are obliged to enter the port from the North or South. Not far from the shore we observe a small island, it is called *Sacrificio*. Attached to this island is a romance familiar to those who remember Prescott's conquest of Mexico by Cortez; here the victims of idolatry and barbarism met their death in a somewhat extraordinary manner. Upon a certain day in each year a youth, selected for his beauty and *physique*, accompanied by his four wives, chosen from the loveliest Aztec flowers of female propriety, were conducted to the island of *Sacrifico*. A priest, who combined the disagreeable attributes of an executioner with those of a consoler, presented himself. He was clothed in blood stained garments; with fiendish dexterity this singular *Padré* cut the young man's heart from its quivering frame and flung it upon an altar which was dyed in the gore of a thousand victims.

We cannot refrain from appreciating the advantages which the present age affords over the unpleasant customs of those days and we pass the island of *Sacrifico* thanking our stars and progression for living in an age which does not ask a greater sacrifice than our purse or a temporary discomfort.

The next point of attraction is the walls of Vera Cruz baked to a dull pink shade. There they lie to the left of us; on our right the fort of *San Juan de Ulloa* lifts its ancient battlements above the reefs and remind us of an old lame watch dog which remains on duty with characteristic fidelity. This fort was commenced in 1569, finished in 1633

INDIAN GOING TO MARKET.

by the Spaniards, in whose power it remained until several years after the Independence of Mexico. It stands upon the spot where Hernando Cortez landed (21st April, 1519); the fort is used as a state prison.

Now a number of boats surround our maritime conveyance and invite us to accept their services to land us individually with our baggage upon the *mole*, a wharf, of which one alone exists for all purposes in the port of Vera Cruz; this wharf consists of a stone pier substantially built in the ancient style of architecture; over this, in rough weather, the capricious waves dash *ad libitum*, in a manner which makes the landing of boats almost equivalent to their wrecking.

The houses of Vera Cruz are constructed to meet any emergency and as experience is a wise instructor, nothing has been omitted to secure them against climatic contingencies to which they are sometimes subjected.

VERA CRUZ—THE PORTAL TO MEXICAN COMMERCE,

INDIAN GOING TO MARKET.

Consists of about 60 acres. It is encompassed by a triangular wall 20 feet high. The population of the city of *The True Cross* is 15,000, of which over 2000 are foreigners. The Indian population predominates in numbers, the Spanish in wealth and influence, though the Mexican is a mixture of both; the streets of Vera Cruz are narrow.

Immense flocks of buzzards constitute the Board of Health and do the street cleaning better than our health departments in the United States; these birds are highly esteemed by the people, more especially because of the small cost they are to the public funds.

Five dollars is the fine imposed on any one who shoots a buzzard; as this bird is not prized by epicures, no one has the desire to hurt them.

Vera Cruz was founded by the Viceroy, Count Monterey at the end of the sixteenth century. It enjoyed the exclusive privilege of receiving importations on Mexican soil until the Declaration of Independence. The city retains all the marks of a past grandeur, which is due to its exceptional position, in a commercial sense ; its massive ramparts bear signs of time and tempest. At present two-thirds of the Mexican commerce passes through this port.

Prior to 1835 the entire carrying trade from this city to the interior was done by mules.

Some of the leading houses do a business of from two to three million dollars a year and the most influential are managed by the German, Spanish and French element. This is the capital of the State of Vera Cruz.

Vera Cruz is situated in the 19° North Latitude and 2° East Longitude from the Mexican meridian. Among the prominent buildings is the Palace. This structure was completed about the year 1627, it is now occupied by the government and police departments. There is also the ancient church of San Francisco, a very fine structure.

The *Plaza del Mercado* is the principal market place ; it cost $90,000 ; there is a fish market *Pescaderia*, and a meat market, *Carniceria*. The *Plaza de la Constitucion* offers the grateful shade and perfume of its luxurious vegetation and is the breathing spot of the city ; it is a square comprising three hundred square feet; in the centre a large bronze fountain which lends its fresh spray to the warm kisses of the torrid breeze and modifies its ardor ; a pleasant place is this to dream at ease. Vera Cruz possesses a school of artillery and an arsenal.

Three hospitals are found in this

POLICEMAN.

city, also a public library. The churches are interesting to visit; among them The Chapel of La Pastora, erected in 1746. The churches of Santo Domingo — I Merced and San Augustin have been closed ever since the war of reform. Some of these structures are used for storing merchandise. A workhouse, the Hospicio de Zamora, affords shelter and occupation to the poor. A well organized police department and in most respects the city is well governed.

We are not importuned at landing by hotel agents as we were in the harbor of Havana; this is accounted for by the fact that there are but few first class hotels in the place. The Hotel Dillegencias and the Hotel Veracruzano are managed by our hospitable friend Dr. Juan who is proverbially attentive to his guests and an excellent caterer. The fare at these hotels is very good, the charge, room with meals and wine, is $2.50 per day.

There are always many "cargadoras" on the look out at the *mole*. These porters will seize your baggage separately, each taking a light charge, and you will be obliged to pay any one who renders you the slightest service. For this reason it will be advisable to place your entire baggage in charge of the boatman and agree upon a price.

On leaving Vera Cruz for the city of Mexico, your baggage will be sent from your hotel, and you will procure your checks and tickets, (the fare being $16 for first class, $12 for second class and $8 for the third class). The trains leave at 11 P. M. The left hand side of the car is the best for sight-seeing. Take upon your arm a heavy overcoat or shawl, as you will need it upon reaching the high lands.

After having reached our hotel and made the necessary disposition with regard to our baggage, &c., the best thing to do is to take a bath; there is nothing so invigorating and pleasant as a bath

PUBLIC PORTER.

after a sea voyage. We enjoy ours in a bath tub constructed of blue and other colored glazed tiles, after which we are prepared to take in every interesting and novel phase of our new quarters. Looking from our window up and down the avenue upon which our hotel is situated, we behold a singular diversity of architecture of color and material; old fashioned cupolas appear on many houses and tiled roofs are the vogue. There are many porches, and white or colored curtains float upon them as screens to hide a Mexican maiden's blush or the inquiring glance of an admiring stranger.

Along the streets perambulate strange men of stranger habits, their movements are adapted to the climate, they *move about* quite leisurely and never appear to be behind time. Strings of mules laden with all manner of merchandise or driven in carts, the sides of which are composed of netting, lend a busy action to the scene; the driver is dressed in a skin jacket braided with silver cord, wears high buff boots, a large gray *sombrero* bound with silver lace and cord, a blood-red *rayah* or waist-belt which forms a bright contrast with the surrounding greens and whites. Here and there velvet eyed *señoritas* are peeping at us through the gaily striped awnings of their balconies. The ladies indulge in cigarettes and do not hide their taste in this respect.

Reclining in their hammocks or in cane chairs, the daughters of Vera Cruz shine through the curling smoke of a fragrant tobacco and laugh at *los Americanos* who gaze upon this charming picture with admiration for the women and surprise at the cigarette.

Let us go to the market place; behold the brilliant assortment of vegetable colors, the bright yellows, the greens, the reds and purples shine in the same light or are modified by the shade of a large parasol an awning or a shed.

TORTILLA MAKER.

The Indian women stretched upon mats in a nonchalant pose, watch their stock of red pepper-pods, tortillas, granadas, or cocoanuts, melons and other fruits.

Rancheros dismounted from their little dapper horses are engaged in marketing. In the open air are shoemakers busily at work ; passing by commercial houses we see merchants and trades people negotiating. There is not a more enterprising set of business people in the country than can be found at Vera Cruz. There is very little work done by day, but at night and far into the morning they can be seen hard at work by candle light.

The *Calle Centrale* is the principal thoroughfare; through it passes a horse railway, the fare is a *real* twelve-and-a half cents. One street runs parallel with the *Calle Centrale* the entire length of the city (about a mile), and two shorter ones fill out the arc that the rear wall makes. Eight or ten cross these at right angles. A bird's eye view of the city reminds us of old Biblical pictures of ancient cities.

WAGONER.

One is amused at the singular names upon business signs: such as " *El Phobre Diabolo,*" (the poor devil), another is "Bueno, Bonito, Barato" (good, pretty, cheap).

We do not find any hacks ; there are no ready conveyances except "shank's mare;" even the fair sex have to foot it. In fact there is not much perambulation going on anyhow. Were it not for the mules and asses this city would be a second Venice. For cleanliness Vera Cruz is proverbial, the streets are cleaner than many American boarding house tables; the baths are unsurpassed.

Sunday is enjoyed here in a sensible manner (in the Latin style), not observed in the old Puritan way.

A stroll to the cemetery may be interesting, the way leads over the almeda or short bridge, across a small stream which is lined with young cocoanut palms. It was here Cortez once built a bridge ten feet or so long for which he charged the Government $3,-000,000, nearly as bad as the Tweed ring. The "Street of Christ" leads out half a mile to the Campo Fonto. The walls of this grave yard are high and deep, tall obelisks stand at their corners. These walls are vaults and contain the sleeping remnants of what was once humanity.

As we proceed on our way to Mexico, in some places we climb four thousand feet in the space of less than 30 miles. Away we go, over the deep gorges of the mountains, on the one side we can almost touch them, on the other, thousands of feet suggest the necessity of traveling with caution. This road is indeed a fine piece of engineering. A Fairlie engine (with an American or English engineer) is puffing away and pulling its very best. This form of engine is well

FRONTIERSMAN.

adapted to the present hard work and steep grades ; the tender is placed on top to add weight to the driving-wheels. The first-class coaches are like those used in Europe and very comfortable. Each coach will seat eight persons.

The first concession for the construction of a railroad from Vera Cruz to Mexico was granted on the 22d of August, 1837, but all manner of impediments prevented it from being completed until 1872, when it was solemnly inaugurated in the presence of the then President Lerdo de Tejada. The road is now known as "La Compañia del Ferrocaril Mexicano." Thus it took 36 years to complete this railroad. Forty presidents served during that time, also one emperor, and it cost the government $12,573,695.00.

On leaving the depot at Vera Cruz the line cuts through the fortifications of the city, crosses the Boulevard de Santiago, passes in sight of the Almeda, the Vera Cruzian promenade, the cemetery of Casa Mata, then across the *lagoon of Cocas*, near the spot where the Vera Cruzian defenders surrendered to General Scott in 1847, then making a sharp turn runs straight some nine miles to Tizeria, the altitude of which is 106 feet above Vera Cruz. The ascent from Vera Cruz to the city of Mexico by rail has been attended with almost exceptional difficulties, yet, as we see, the feat has been accomplished.

Before reaching the central table lands, the railroad climbs three immense natural steps which have to be mounted : the first from Vera Cruz to the foot of the Chiquihuite mountain, the second to El Infiernillo, and the third to Boca del Monte, a distance of 172½ kilometres from Vera Cruz and a total ascent of 7,924 feet above the level of the sea. One of the ravines, most difficult to cross, was that of Metlac, situated between Cordova and Orizaba. Trains commenced running from Vera Cruz to Orizaba, on the 5th of September 1872. thanks to the indefatigable energy of the engineer corps, of which Ner Buchanan was the chief.

CAVALRYMAN.

As regards engineering the Vera Cruz rail-road is unsurpassed, and the grandeur of scenery along its route will remain in our memory as an exceptional and admirable picture ; one can scarcely form an idea of this glorious panorama, rising as we do from the rippling waters of the shore, which chant their melodies through shells and pebbles, we glide away upon the even rail through forests of fragrant vegetation and gigantic trees, and then through caves into the bright sunlight. Now passing over a marvel 'of architecture, that unites two prominent points, and overcomes the almost unsurmountable depths of ravines, which bathe their flowers in serpentine rivulets below, and then away we fly into the clouds to gaze upon nature in minature ; at times our heart is in our mouth, while casting a glance into indefinite chasms. As we approach the city of Mexico, we are met by an express agent, who will take charge of our baggage, keys and checks, and give us a receipt therefor ; his charge is twenty-five cents per package, and he will deliver our affairs at our hotel ; these agents are entirely responsible. Among the best hotels in the city of Mexico, we find the *Hotel Iturbide*, (the late pa:ace of the Emperor Iturbide), this is the finest hotel in the city, and contains about 400 rooms, the rate of board being from fifty cents to three dollars a day, meals a la carte. The restaurant is kept by Dn. Carlos Recamier, and an excellent repast costs but one dollar, and arrangements can be made with the restaurant by the week. This hotel is the resort of Americans ; the attendance is good and the proprietor always on the *qui-vive* for the comfort of his guests. The hotels Gillow, San Carlos, Bella Union, and National, are also to be recommended; they are situated on prominent thoroughfares and as in the majority of cases in the city of Mexico, the meals are à la carte, the attendance good, and prices moderate. Our travelers must not forget that here, as in Cuba, the servants expect a fee; it insures better service; and every body subscribes to the custom (un medio), about six cents of our money is a suitable fee. In Paris some restaurants pay their hands entirely

SERVANT.

by fees, if a waiter receives any money he deposits it in a large money box, every evening the proprietor declares a dividend in proportion to the number of servants and extent of the cash in the fee box.

Montezunema was particularly fond of a certain fish (the red mullet); he had them brought to Mexico city by means of slaves, who would run very swiftly in short relays from Vera Cruz. This fish is very highly prized by epicures, it is in fact very delicious, and the Mexicans understand how to prepare it. The red mullet is to Mexico what terrapins are to Philadelphia.

THE CITY OF MONTEZUMA.

Those who remember Prescott's work the Conquest of Mexico by Hernando Cortez, will recognize in our sketches the premises at least of our travels, they will recall to mind those interesting pages in which the great author dwells upon Aztec grandeur and Spanish conquerors.

But here we will deal with present scenes and issues, and consign to our leisure moments that which the past has consummated. The Mexico of to-day, is our present subject. This *promised land* of our American commerce embraces an extent of 856,000 square miles, equal to France, Germany and Austria, added together. Its population is 9,000,000, its resources inexhaustible, its climate diversified and its commerce restricted to the limits of a small carrying trade.

When railroads have been laid throughout Mexico the exports from that country will surprise the world. Within a few years only have the Mexicans shown their disposition to embark largely in extensive pursuits. The

WAITER.

valley in which the city of Mexico stands is 45 miles long, 35 miles wide, and containing 700,000 inhabitants; the temperature fluctuates between 70° to 50° Fahrenheit. The longest day is thirteen hours and fifty minutes; the population of the city of Mexico is 250,000.

Let us take ourselves to our Hotel, after making a change in our apparel and refreshing ourselves as best we can, a stroll down the *Calle Plate-*

ros may not be uninteresting; this is the Broadway of Mexico, and we would add that it resembles the New York Broadway in one particular alone, which is, that the way *is not broad at all.*

This street leads from the *Almeda* to the *Plaza Mayor*, there is at all hours great activity upon this thoroughfare, on either side of which very irregular architecture is spread from the aristocratic mansion blue-tiled, gold-balconied, scarlet-blinded, to the dingy flat roofed, two storied stone front. Each block has a different name. The *Calle Plateros* or rather the street which bears this name and a thousand others in company is lined with stores, which have a second class Parisian appearance, the goods exposed therein bear the French trade mark in a majority of instances. Here we find the *Café Concordia*, the -Delmonico of Mexico; we stop a moment to refresh ourselves with a sorbet or a cobler.

At the corner of the streets Indians in picturesque costumes

VENDER OF REFRESHMENTS.

offer to sell us large bouquets of violets, we should say an immense bouquet, for the small sum of 25 cents, where in New York the same would cost not less than $10. The ladies here seldom venture in the street on foot; they drive a shopping and visiting.

THE POPULATION.

We find that the Indians are by far the best part of the population. After the whites, there are three distinct classes:

First, the whites descended from the original Spaniards, or from French, German, or English ancestors; second, the pure Indians; and thirdly, the *Mestizos*, or mixed race, who constitute the laboring class. Estimating the present population at 10.000.000, the whites will probably number 2,000,000 —20%—, the Indians 3,500,000—35%— and the *Mestizos* 4,500,000—45%. The Indians belong to various tribes and differ as much among themselves in every peculiarity as do the Anglo-Saxons from the Latin race.

The Indians of the cities are low and brutal, constantly drunk. In some parts of the country, however, they are hard working and industrious, neat in their person and sober in their habits. In the mining districts they prove by far the best hands and command the highest wages, they are very religious and superstitious and they appear to blend in their articles of faith the Christian and Pagan dogmas in a most singular manner.

MEXICAN SERVANT.

It is an unfortunate fact that the white and Indian elements are rapidly becoming numerically less, while the Mestizo element is increasing. The Indian women are wonderfully addicted to maternity and commence these duties as early as 14 years of age, but notwithstanding their prolific peculiarities, the Indian element is rapidly dying out through the ravages of various diseases, exposure, bad nourishment and hard work. Of the Aztec arts and sciences nothing remains, excepting the manufacture of feather birds and rag-statues. The manner in which the Indians pluck the feathers from live birds would inspire our philanthropical friend Mr. Bergh with a sanguine indignation.

The *Mestizos* constitute the producing or agricultural element, the small shopkeepers, the politicians, they are generally undersized, with copper colored skins and straight hair. They possess neither the energy of the whites nor the working qualities of the pure Indians, they are inordinately fond of *Palque*, the national beverage, *pulque* is to the *Mestizos* what *lager* is to the *Germans*; it is distilled from the Maguey plant, has the color of thick milk and is not bad to take when one becomes accustomed to it. It costs a mere song, something like 6 cents a gallon, and even at that price there is a fair profit in the sale; for this reason the most fertile and productive lands are given up to the culture of the *Maguey*. This plant often takes 10 years to come to perfection, it requires very little cultivation; the *Mestizos* not only cultivate the *Maguey* but are its principal consumers and the consequence is not favorable to the physical, nor mental parts of the Mestizos race. This beverage has upon the system an enervating effect; taken in moderation, however, it is an excellent tonic; in quantities, it is fearful in its consequences.

PUBLIC LETTER WRITER.

There are as many *pulque* mills in the city of Mexico as there are *gin* mills in New York; as we freely criticise our own bad habits, we feel warranted in being entirely frank with regard to what we consider a danger to the Mexican nation. It is estimated that the consumption of pulque amounts to a pint for each inhabitant in the city of Mexico, 250,000 pints or 31 000 gallons every day.

A pulque drunk lasts twenty-four hours. A plant produces about four quarts of pulque per day, and lasts six months, so that the possessor of a small patch of ground can raise *maguey* and remain in a semi-intoxicated condition (which many do), for the balance of their days.

The *Calle Plateros* has its sidewalks lined with vehicles of an ancient and clumsy model; here as in Havana, the salesmen are obliged to carry their wares to the carriages. In the afternoon a drive on the Paseo is quite the

MEXICAN GENTLEMAN.

style for those who can "ride in chaises," but, as the Irishman remarked, the poor people "walk by them," (the chaises).

Strange sights are witnessed upon this occasion. *Haciendados* and *Ran- cheros* in their broad brimmed *sombreros* and leather *chaquetas* jackets and silver frogged breeches, through the outside seam of which, loosely roll white flowing drawers, swaggering along the sidewalk, their great spurs jingling, and their silver ornaments dangling. Indios trotting onward, the man bearing live stock and fruit in a wicker frame, upon his forehead. And the woman with her baby slung in the folds of her blue rebozo, both arms engaged in carrying provisions.

Water carriers, fruit sellers, soldiers followed by their wives, managing *tortillas*. Mules and asses driven by half naked men and boys, their feet, baked by the burning roads to an ash white, and their limbs bronzed by the sun. *Muchachos* bearing furniture upon their heads. A demure *Señorita* clad in the picturesque mantilla; swells in short-tailed coats, high-heeled boots and narrow-rimmed hats puff away at their cigarettes through silver holders, companies of foot-soldiers shuffling along in sandals, *guacharez;* civil guards trotting

WATER CARRIER.

on thoroughbreds, in buff and steel with sword and matchlock, recalling the days of Cromwell's ironsides, and occasionally a troop of cavalry such as Bazaine loved to lead in Africa. These are the sights or some of them which attract our attention and excite a continued interest and curiosity.

The *Plateros* leads to the *Plaza Mayor*, this plaza is the grand square of the city. Its shape is oblong, 270 yards long by 200 feet wide. Its northern side is entirely occupied by the cathedral and sagario; upon the side of which once stood the Aztec pyramid and temple. Cortez, after destroying these Indian monuments, gave the ground to the Franciscan monks who built thereon a cathedral which was demolished in 1530. The present edifice was commenced in 1573 and completed in 1667, at an expense to the crown of Spain of $1,762,000; the towers were not completed until 1791 by Damien Ortiz, an American architect, at a cost of $194,000. The basis of its columns are cut out of the Aztec idols found in *Teocalli.* This cathedral measures from north to south 426 feet and from east to west 200 feet; the height of the roof being 175 feet and the towers 25 feet higher.

The *Sagario* is too florid to command more than artistic comment. Laid in the wall at a height of five feet we perceive the famous Aztec calendar, carved out of one solid block of basalt; it weighs 25 tons, its diameter being twelve feet six inches. It is supposed to have been constructed in 1279. With this calendar the Mexicans inherit the system of Toltec astronomy.

Upon the eastern side of the Plaza stands the *Palacio del Gobierno.* *Los Portales de Merca-*

BIRD SELLER.

deras, a row supported by a colonnade appears upon the western side of the plaza; and upon the south we see the municipal chamber, *Casa de Cabildo.* A lovely mass of vegetation, including trees in perpetual verdancy and delicious flower beds, marble fountains and seats form the bouquet that graces the centre of the *Plaza Mayor*; an excellent orchestra, such as Theodore Thomas might be proud to lead, gives nightly concerts.

The *Palacio del Gobierno* was constructed by Cortez, one of its rooms can contain 3,000 people. In this palace are the President's official apartments and offices, the cabinets of the ministry, the headquarters of the military commander, a barrack, the treasury and archives of the nation.

La *Plaza Santo Domingo* is an interesting part of the city. The old church of the same name, with its pink walls and glittering tiled dome faces

PLAZA AND CATHEDRAL BY MOONLIGHT.

the south; on the east stands the school of medicine—the curriculum is seven long years—and that terror to importers, the custom house; on the west of the plaza an arcade shelters old scriveners who earn a livelihood by scratching all sorts of communications for the illiterate; every conceivable writing, from a love-letter to a last will and testament, and all for *un media*. The building, now occupied by the school of medicine, was formerly the seat of the inquisition tribunal, which was suppressed in 1813, then it was used as a state prison. The notable "Yard of the Oranges" was situated within the walls of this Mexican "Bastille." It has since been used as a lottery office, a barrack and a house of congress. In 1854 it was adapted to its present purposes, having been purchased for $50,286.

The People Engaged in Business,

such as bankers and merchants do not run themselves to death as they do in the United States; the Mexicans follow the example of the Europeans in this particular: at eight the merchant opens his store, at twelve he closes it

NIGHT WATCHMAN.

and devotes three hours to a *déjeuné à la fourchette*, as the French term the 12 o'clock breakfast, and to digesting it. The consequence is favorable to the digestive apparatus and dyspepsia does not trouble the Mexican stomach. From 3 to 4 o'clock the business of the day is completed (we allude to the wholesale trade and banking houses). The Germans have almost the entire control of the banking business which was formerly done exclusively by English houses. The majority of the best shopkeepers are German, Spanish and French. The best clubs are the French and German casinos, both of which have large memberships, and the balls and fetes which they give about every month are simply magnificent.

"Those who visit Rome should do as do the Romans," this proverb is equally applicable in our estimation to all quarters of the globe. Not only should a traveler endeavor to follow the customs of the sphere in which he holds a temporary or transient position, but he should also avoid, as much as possible, to excite the ill will or prejudice of the people whom he visits, by political or religious differences of opinion. Prudence as well as good breeding will, we believe, guide the traveler in this respect and suggest to him a discreet and amiable deportment upon foreign premises. It is customary in Mexico to offer a guest everything which he may require for his comfort and convenience and literally to put the entire house and everything in it at his disposal for the time being. This practice grows out of a genuine feeling of liberality and hospitality; but the language used is such as to be quite readily misunderstood by a stranger who measures expressions by the cold matter-of-fact rule among Americans, who attach no more weight to a mere formality than it is justly entitled to. When you enter the house of a friend or even a person to whom you have a letter of introduction, he at once tells you that you are in your own house and that you are the master and he your guest or something to that effect; he really expects you to make yourself at home but on the other hand pays you the compliment of supposing that you have at least an ordinary amount of common sense and will know o ugh of what constitutes the rules and customs of society not to abuse the offer and outstay your welcome.

A visit to the Academy of San Carlos will compensate the artist and

FLOWER GIRL.

amateurs of pictures generally. They will find a collection which (if we may take Mexican opinion as an authority) is the best on the American continent. The suburbs of Mexico are not like those of Orizaba, yet the rock and grove

RURAL SOLDIER.

of Chapultepec deserve our consideration. Just where the houses end stands the equestrian statue of Charles IV. of Spain; it is regarded by critics as one of the most successful efforts in this line of art. From this point also is the *Calzada de la Reforma*, a drive which leads us to Chapultepec, which looks in the distance not unlike Windsor Castle, when viewed from the other end of the famous Long Walks. Here, in the afternoons, all Mexicans turn out to drive in carriages or ride on horseback. The carriages are almost exclusively of French manufacture, are generally close with the exception of a few Victorias; this singular fact is explained by the desire to have a suitable conveyance during the three months of rain which prevails in this climate.

We will now observe the equestrians when mounted *à l'Anglaise*, they are dressed *à l'Anglaise*, but if they mount a Mexican horse the entire paraphernalia is of Mexican fashion ; both the horse and man are harnessed in a somewhat artistic, but, rather comfortable style. It will not be necessary to describe a Mexican saddle and bridle, nor will we sketch again the *sombrero*, the jacket, pants and enormous spurs of the cavalier.

Half way between the statue of Charles IV. and Chapultepec is a "circle," in the middle of which appears the statue of Christopher Columbus ; at this point the view of two volcanos in the pink atmosphere of a setting sun is truly grand. The palace, which was erected in 1785 upon the very spot which Montezuma's place occupied, is now an astronomi-

FRUIT SELLER.

cal observatory, and, like most public buildings here, is not in the very best repair. Still the view is sublime; there in the distance the valley of Mexico, with its lakes and green waving fields of rich vegetation, its fringe of mountains that are veiled in a blue atmosphere, and the various transparent tints

that radiate upon the heaven's mists to reflect their colors upon nature's flowery bosom. The water supply of Mexico was formerly brought to the city through the celebrated aqueduct; now there are water pipes, and the ancient conduit that afforded a clear and wholesome stream is being removed as an old and incapacitated servant.

Molino del Rey lies not far from Chapultepec, let us see that too, and just beyond lies *Tacubaya*, a fashionable suburb and country seat of wealthy Mexicans; here we visit the military school which was formerly situated at Chapultepec.

The city of Mexico is supplied with two kinds of water, namely "*agua delgada*," soft water, and "*agua gorda*," thick water; the first flows from springs in the southern part of the city, near the foot of the mountains; the second has its source at Chapultepec. Two very large aqueducts store the *agua delgada* and *agua gorda*, one at each side of the city. There are also many artesian wells, which are used for domestic purposes. Before the rainy season the sewers of Mexico are emptied. There are many excellent tramways in the city, the management of which is very different from that of our American horse railroads; for instance the driver is permitted to recline at ease in a comfortable arm chair, while the conductor takes it as leisurely as possible, smokes his cigarette, and not infrequently asks a passenger for a light. In a Mexican tramway the drivers and conductors are men and the horses and mules are beasts, but in New York the reverse seems to exist in consequence of Mr. Bergh's supervision and the indifference which corporations exhibit toward their human employees. The waiters in Mexico are not less impudent than they are in Paris, but if you fee them suitably they will assume a respectful attitude at least while they serve you, that is why we recommend the fee system. The fare at most of the restaurants is good and the *cuisine* French. There is plenty of pork, but it is allowed to go to waste, they are not up to the art of knowing how to cure it for hams. American hams can be found everywhere and sell at seventy-five cents per pound. The poultry is good, game and meat of all kinds is excellent, and is well served; the *tortola*, however, made from corn ground fine between two stones and flattened in the hands to a thin cake of oval shape, makes an excellent *salmi*. Wines, Liquors and all drinks are as good as they are in New York, and at much cheaper prices. American and German breweries are being introduced, but beer sells at such a high price that it is not yet within the reach of the class of people who would consume largely; a bottle of St. Louis lager beer sells for 36 cents, and some German lager sells at 50 cts. per bottle. English ales can be had at 25 cts. per bottle, but the Mexicans don't take to it. You will experience a decided physical and moral improvement by the change, although of course we recommend moderation in diet, as well as in all human pursuits.

Mexico city is a paradise of climates, the air is just right every day throughout the year; an overcoat in the morning and evening will be found very comfortable. English, French and German is very generally spoken.

A Few Remarks about Money Matters.

The silver dollar is the only legal tender in Mexico. In the city of Mexico the bank notes of the "London Bank of Mexico and South America" pass everywhere *at par*, but in other cities and in the country they are not accepted except at a usurious discount. As it is neither convenient nor safe to carry large sums in silver, if you intend to travel in the interior, we advise you to provide yourself with a circular letter of credit on the various offices of the diligence. There is at present a scheme on foot to establish a National Bank of Mexico, with English capital, and to make its notes a legal tender.

The Tivoli Gardens.

The Tivoli Gardens open on the Avenue of *San Cosme* just below the terminus of an ancient aqueduct, here one can enjoy a very excellent repast under the trees or in their branches as tables and benches are placed in these aerial shades. The Tivoli Gardens are the resort, which the *beau monde* of Mexico frequent, when a dinner or a supper *al fresca* is proposed. One can pass many a pleasant hour in these delicious shades, where nature and a good bill of fare are so harmoniously blended.

Apropos of horseback riding it might to said that, very few Mexican gentlemen are not expert in that accomplishment. There is however a very decided difference between our English style of riding and the Mexican modus operandi, in the first place their horses are small, they pace or canter, and their saddles are comfortable chairs. Those who are familiar with our small smooth English saddles, and open stirrups, our tall high action trotters can appreciate the difference between Mexican riding and American riding.

If you want to have a good time, my friend, take to the Mexican horse.

EMPEDADRILLO STREET CITY OF MEXICO

In Mexico you can stand in your stirrups, or lay back in your comfortable saddle, the horse will carry you along smoothly, no jockeying (or rising in your saddle) is necessary. We ride more after the style of the Indian with bent knees pressing the horse and bearing but slightly upon our stirrups.

The Mexican holds his legs straight and often stands upon his stirrups which are large boxes made of wood. After partaking of a cup of coffee start in the early morning for a ride, the *Almeda* is passed, not, however, without our questioning its dark thickets with suspicious glances in search of some robber.

The "Mad-woman's drive" or "Empress Drive" as it is now styled is much frequented by equestrians, the celebrated tree of Montezuma stands at the end of an ancient grove and is well worth a visit. This tree is a gigantic specimen, many hundred years have witnessed the growth of this vegetable patriarch, which has stood so proudly in defiance of earthquake, cyclone and inundation.

Further on we come to the bath of Montezuma where a refreshing bath may be enjoyed, passing on for a mile or so we admire many elegant country seats, groves, ravines, rivulets, lakelets, mounds, flowers in profusion, tall Australian gum trees, sumptuous houses with their large courts open to visitors, encircled with flowers, sedans, and pictures.

Now by leaving the city from the south western gate, we make for the canal; this body of water is worth visiting, it is the feeder of the city ; upon its surface the market boats plow their indolent way to the capital; for five hundred years it has served as a conduit to feed the population of Mexico city. On it the boats are propelled by hand ; we see flat boats loaded with truck, fruits, hay and oats, pleasure boats well patronized ply the waters, it is almost a Venice. These canals have villages along their banks, some of which rise to the dignity of the towns.

Among the curiosities peculiar to Mexico, the Floating Gardens are not the least interesting, these singular formations of ground that float in the canals at irregular intervals form truckgardens, which yield vegetables and fruit the year around ; of course the perfect irrigation of these gardens need not be questioned.

The statue of the graceful Montezuma is still in the quarries, but as the Aztecs are not yet extinct, and in view of the fact that the last President was a pure Aztec, as are many of the present leaders in Mexico, we may hope to see even at this late day a statue to that renowned monarch. It is

MARKET PLACE IN THE CITY OF MEXICO.

safe to say that few persons will in that case be able to criticise the likeness. After we have seen Mexico, a visit to some of the principal cities in its vicinity will be found very interesting and without which one can never know what Mexico or its people are. The first place to visit, will be

CUERNVACA,

situated from Mexico city in a south easterly direction ; we take the stage coach, which leaves every day from the Hotel Iturbide in the rear court yard. This city is a perfect garden of Eden ; the distance is short and the ride will be found full of sights; elegant residences appear on the roadside, and we can see the house which was once the resort of Carlotta and Maximilian, and although in decay is still full of rare luxuries. Vistas and trees and bowers and flowers, bananas, cocoa and other palms, oranges, lemons, mangos, coffee and all manner of precious fruits abound. Cuernvaca can boast of one of the largest and most interesting market places in Mexico, where may be had fruit of every kind, vegatables of all sorts at prices which would gladden the eye of a New York boarding house keeper. After visiting the churches of which there are a number, we return to our hotel and the next morning seek the friendship of our stage coach and again we roll on to the capital.

A VISIT TO PUEBLA.

The *Puebla* branch starts from *Apizaco*. It was inaugurated on the 16th of September, 1869 by the President of the Republic, who was then *Don Benito Juarez*. From *Apizaco* the railroad continues south east to the station of *Santa Anna Chiantempam*, at 159 kilometres from Mexico city and 75 kilometres from Apizaco; this station has an altitude of 2,400 metres above the sea. The next station is *Panzacola*, at about the same altitude. Near this place is an extensive iron foundry. Puebla, the capital of the State of the same name, is situated at 221 kilometres from Mexico city and 47 from *Apizaco* in a valley, the western extremity of which is guarded by the night sentinels. *Popocatepete* and *Ixtaccihuate* by Orizaba and the *Cofre de Perote* to the north east and the *Matinche* to the north. This valley is rich in grain and is watered by the river Atoyac which passes through the suburbs of Puebla city and empties into the Pacific Ocean. Over this river is an elegant iron bridge. The city is remarkably clean, has straight and regular thoroughfares and presents

NATIONAL PALACE IN THE CITY OF MEXICO.

rather a monumental appearance. Among the remarkable structures are the cathedral *San Francisco*, the *Guerrero* theatre, and the *Compania*.

Puebla was founded in 1531 by Spaniards and Indian women about 50 in number. Now it is the elegant and aristocratic abode of some of the wealthiest citizens of Mexico. An active trade is carried on in cotton and woolen manufactures, as well as earthen ware, glass, cutlery and soap, and promises rapid developments in a near future. The markets are supplied with the choicest products of Mexico at very moderate prices. Our hotel was once a college or theological school; over the gateway may be seen the singular initials I. II. S. The churches in Puebla are grander than those of Mexico city, its convents and ecclesiastical institutions more numerous and wealthy. The streets are paved in broad blocks, that shine in their cleanliness; here as in other Mexican cities the drainage is done from the centre of the streets. There are above 60,000 people. The fields appear in better cultivation than those which surround the city of Mexico. Irrigation is easy as the mountains near by keep the streams from becoming ry.

A visit to the cathedral will compensate the tourist, it is adorned with pictures and statues, railings, and other ornaments of gold and silver. A splendid view of the city and surrounding country can be had from its top— the door leading to the tower next to the Plaza Mayor is always open, visitors are allowed to enter at any and all times—the view from there is beyond description, the landscape is one that once seen is never to be forgotten. A plain lies on the right about 100 miles in length by 90 in breadth; at each corner stand the magnificient mountains, of which Mexico is famed, unequalled in heighth or grandeur by the highest alps. Twenty-five miles to the southwest stands the mighty volcanic peak of Popocatepetl or the smoking mountain, the fires that so long throbbed within its breast slumbering after thousands of centuries of activity; its head is now covered with snow. There is an enormous amount of sulphur taken out of the extinct crater, and the carrying down of this and the frozen snow on the sides of the mountain employs hundreds of Indians. Popocatepetl is the very beau ideal of a volcano, and we advise all who visit Puebla not to forget to pay it a visit. The best way of reaching it is by taking any of the public coaches, and if possible, supply yourself with a guide; there are plenty who are reliable, and for a trifling sum will accompany you.

Another of the sights around Puebla not less interesting then Popocatepetl is the great pyramid of Cholula, it is indeed a wonderful remnant of an

METLAC BRIDGE ON THE MEXICO & VERA CRUZ R. R.

extinct civilization; it lies about seven miles to the east of Puebla, and is reached in about an hour and a half ride in a public coach; the road to Cholula is so bad that it requires four horses to drag the coach along. When Cortez invaded Mexico he found Cholula, the great city of temples, whither all Mexico was wont to repair, so much so that he said it reminded him of a European town, there were so many beggars in the streets. A sure test, according to him, of civilization, it is said that at the time of the conquest there were 150,000 inhabitants—now it is only one long strappling street with a small plaza nicely laid out with flowers of which the Indians and *mestizos* are very fond. The pyramid or teocalli (house of God) of Cholula is supposed to be the largest in the world. Its length is 1423 feet, its perpendicular height 177 feet and its base. which is square, covers nearly forty-four acres ; in shape it is a truncated cone, the area of the truncated summit being over an acre. In Cholula many old Indian women are met with who ask you to buy pottery goods; in addition to the peddlers of goods, there are also many stores where a large collection of goods and numerous specimens of the astic pottery are sold; the prices asked are generally very high, the tourist will be careful in his offers for it can be bought at half the price asked ; they will ask a price and before you have a chance to say whether you will take it or not ask you how much you will give.

A VISIT TO THE MINING DISTRICTS.

Pachuca is situated in the State of Hidalgo, north east from the city of Mexico; a visit to this mining town will amply compensate our traveler. Pachuca can be reached by two routes, but as yet no railroad communication has been made to it; we are consequently obliged to travel in *diligencias;* only those who have already experienced the peculiarities of this style of traveling can appreciate its various phases. We take the stage or *diligencia* at *Ometusco,* a station on the Vera Cruz and Mexico railroad; the diligencia runs only three times a week. The second line runs from Cuantitlan, on the Vera Cruz railroad; they start at seven o'clock A. M. Here we are supplied with an excellent cup of coffee; while we indulge in this early breakfast, the mules are being harnessed to the diligencia. The driver is worthy of note with his tight leather trousers, ornamented with rows of silver buttons, his short cut roundabout à la mode " bull fight," and his large white *sombrero;* he cuts a bold figure and drives excellently; by his side an assistant is serving his ap-

MEXICAN FANDANGO

prenticeship. Hanging on each side of the coach we perceive quite an assortment of whips of various sizes and weights, devoted to the service of each respective mule; besides these instruments of torture a collection of stones may be seen behind the driver's assistant who pelts the foremost mules which cannot be reached with the whip. When night sets in this assistant runs ahead of the team with a pine torch in each hand. Behind the driver is the *pescante;* we prefer this position, which is the cheapest, to the garlicy and pulque atmosphere of the inside. At last all is ready, the mules are set at liberty and away we go rattling over the pavements, until we strike the main road to Pachuca. On either side of us broad fields of wheat and corn, and *maguey* meet our gaze. The natives are plowing with very primitive appliances and oxen that move like snails. This picture is bordered with mountains in the horizon which resemble clouds of a neutral tint; we are now traveling through dust only about a foot thick. Every half hour we pass an Indian village with its two or three fine churches and its miserable huts, built of unbaked bricks. At about one o'clock we reach the little town, where we partake of a modest breakfast, after which we resume our journey and arrive at *Pachuca* at six P. M.

The Aztecs worked the mines of Pachuca long before the Spaniards became possessors of the country. The production of silver is enormous. In 1557 Medina introduced the process of amalgamating silver ore with quicksilver and volatizing the later, and the first experiments were made at the mines of Pachuca. Born introduced this process in Europe in 1750.

The population of Pachuca is about 13,000, of which 5,000 are engaged in mining. The captains of the mines being generally Cornishmen, one might imagine himself in an English town. You see one hotel styled "The Port of Liverpool," another "The Three Navies." You can call for roast beef rare and a glass of Bass on draught. The Real del Monte Company works most of the mines; under Señor Landero, president, the company has extensive reducing works. In the Santo Gertrude's mine recently a very rich vein was struck, the yield being $500,000 a year; the shares of this stock selling a short time ago at a dollar, are now quoted at $900! The operations in mining as well as the apparatus used for the purpose are exceedingly primitive. It is fair to calculate that with our improved machinery at least one hundred per cent. more ore could be taken from these mines. The fact is, that every pound of ore is elevated in leather bags or cow skins by means of an ordinary windlass. The stock of a Mexican mine is divided into twenty-five *bars;* one belongs to the government; six, known as free shares, to the discoverer, and the others are placed upon the market for sale. No dividend is paid upon the free shares until the money expended as working capital to start has been repaid to the original subscribers.

Let us Visit Orizaba.

In Orizaba there is no fever; it is situated 4,027 feet above the level of the sea; the average temperature is 72° Fahrenheit. The town has 13,000 inhabitants ; it is old and of quaint appearance, the streets straight but irregular, houses with overhanging tiled roofs; as in Vera Cruz, the sewers or gutters run in the centre of the streets ; generally the houses have only one story. As this city is situated upon a railroad line it has outstripped its rivals, Jalapa and Cuernavaca. Some of the finest estates in the world are perched upon these hills; the sun casts its amorous rays upon the most lovely spot that nature has conceived. Orizaba is a very Eden, a rose fallen from Heaven and held in the embrace of mighty mountains among which the ice-capped volcano stands as sovereign. Here we are in a lovely valley at an altitude of 4,000 feet above the sea, at the very foot of the old volcano which the Aztecs called *Citlaltepatl* or Star Mountain.

Orizaba presents the appearance of a magnificent garden; it is a delightful spot to visit. Here we find the principal stoneyards and work shops of the Vera Cruz R. R. Of late years Orizaba has come into especial prominence; at the railway depot there is collected quite a colony of English and American people and to hear English spoken is no novelty; there has also been established lately an American missionary school, a branch of that at Mexico City.

The French army under Bazaine had its headquarters here. It was also at Orizaba that Maxamillian held the famous council after the French evacuation of Mexico, to determine whether he should abdicate or not. We know that he determined to remain and we also know that that resolution sealed his death warrant. The proprietor of the hotel at Orizaba at present is an ex-lieutenant in poor Maximillian's army.

A trip to Cordova is a good diversion for three or four hours; stages run from Orizaba to this place. Cordova lies 2000 feet lower than Orizaba; the scenery is truly grand, the gorgeous coloring of the flowers and shrubs, banana trees, upon which rich fruit hang in clusters, and the golden orange trees, prolific in their juicy product, all meet the eye and bring water to the mouth of the least fastidious.

The coffee plant which grows wild reaches colossal proportions and lines the side of our route. Every now and then our conveyance which resembles a diligence, on a rough scale, makes a spurt ahead down the road or flies over a rustic wooden bridge at a fine rate of speed. Now we pass the famous *Barranca* of Metlac, where the railroad crosses. This railroad bridge is a marvel of engineering skill. The grade at either end is three feet in the hundred, and the radius of the curve is three hundred and twenty-five feet, the passengers in the first car look across to the opposite hill and see the last cars running exactly parallel. Close to the Metlac Barranca runs the little river Jonso, the waters of which pass through the Mount Sumidero and conceal their virginity in its fragrant forests.

About a mile from Cordova we may visit the residence and coffee plantation of an enthusiastic German botanist; the introduction of coffee into this region is of recent date, but the production is already very large; the coffee plant is an evergreen, it will, if improved, grow to the height of thirty feet; the leaves are dark and shining, of an oblong shape. This plant is kept down by pruning to about 5 feet so that its substance may be conveyed to the fruit, and constant attention is bestowed upon the ground in which it grows to keep it clear from weeds. The coffee plant is started in nurseries, planted out at a year old and bear fruit after three years growth, but not in perfection until the fifth year. Cordova is sixty-five miles from Vera Cruz and sixteen miles from Orizaba.

From Vera Cruz to Jalapa.

This route is divided into two branches, to the west of *Tejeria*. One branch traverses the heights of *Chiquihuite* and *Maltrata* mountains, and unites *Vera Cruz* with Orizaba, Cordova and Mexico; we have already gone over it on our way to the capital. The other reaches the central table land by the route of Jalapa and Perote; our attention will now be given to this route. After reaching the "*Paso de San Juan,*" the line follows a most picturesque tract of country. Our cars are open and permit our admiring observations to roam on all sides over the charming beauty of a luxuriant vegetation which exhales its perfume toward the grand azure of the heavens. Large flocks of birds, resplendent in their plumage, chatter away like so many young girls at a tea party. What are they talking about? might be asked : perhaps they are criticising us.

At all events they appear very busy and excited, flying here and there from the tall palm trees to the lesser vegetation ; this scene is different from that which we have observed on our road to Puebla. The country here is wild and almost abandoned to the birds and beasts of its virgin forests, few cultivated fields meet our gaze, seldom do we pass one of those small hamlets that indicate the presence of man and the pursuit of agriculture.

Over this country in long years past the trade between the city of Mexico and Vera Cruz did its transportation, now it is almost abandoned. Jalapa is situated at the foot of the basaltic mountain, Macuiltepete, in a delightful spot; the convent of San Francisco, not far from the city has the appearance of a fortress, from its cupolas an extended view of the rich country which surrounds Jalapa may be enjoyed. Jalapa has an altitude of 1,320 metres.

This romantic spot has been compared very properly, to a bouquet of flowers on a couch of green tapestry. In fact the entire atmosphere is perfumed and the traveler receives intimation of his approach to this city through the medium of the breeze long before he treads the flower-fields of Jalapa. The climate here is temperate, we find ourselves 1.320 metres having travelled 114 kilometres, all in the space of 10 hours.

The population is about 11,000, at present the state authorities and the bishopric of Vera Cruz reside at Jalapa. It was here that Santa Anna first proclaimed the Republic. As we enter the principal street of this city we perceive the Palace of the state authorities, an elegant structure sustained by doric arches, it is situated on the south side of a *Plaza* forming the terminus to the principal thoroughfare. The people of Jalapa are as hospitable and kind as we have found them generally in our Mexican peregrinations.

The principal agricultural products here are coffee, tobacco, vanilla, cotton, jalap root, and grain. The cost of cotton landed at Vera Cruz from this place is 14 cents per pound, valuable mines and quarries are found but have not been worked to any important extent.

A Visit to Tlacotalpan.

This is a beautiful city, situated on the left bank of the Papaloapan and opposite the conjunction of this river with that of San Juan, in the State of Vera Cruz; the trade is considerable, and the industry well advanced. The women of this place are considered singularly handsome and remarkable for the beauty and expression of their eys and complexion of their skin.—The city has a principal square and fine promenades. Tlacotalpan is a city of progress and promises in a greater degree than any other on the coast to become the New Orleans of the Mexican Republic. The means of reaching this place is very convenient; an American built side wheel steamer of 600 tons capacity, runs between Vera Cruz and that place, and leaves twice a week. The passage rates are $16.00 for an excursion. The steamer has a capacity for carrying eighty passengers; the distance from Tlacotalpan to Vera Cruz is sixty miles.

After having visited the different places of Mexico to which we have referred in our brief sketches, the tourist has two ways of returning to New York. By way of Havana, or by steamer from Vera Cruz to New Orleans. By this route one can return to New York six days and a half after leaving Vera Cruz, calculating four days from Vera Cruz to New Orleans and two and a half days from New Orleans to New York. This mode of returning from Mexico is the quickest and has much favor with tourists. The trip up the Mississippi River is very interesting ; its length—120 miles—is made in about 12 hours. The river on either side is lined with sugar plantations and orange groves. Although the route via New Orleans may be preferred by some, the other way of returning via Havana is equally agreeable to those who wish to avoid railroad travel.

The Steamship Company of Messrs. F. Alexandre & Sons issue excursion tickets, good on either route.

LAWS OF MEXICO REGARDING PASSENGERS AND THEIR BAGGAGE.

ARTICLE 80 OF THE TARIFF.—The following rules will be observed in the Custom Houses of the Republic for the disembarkment of passengers and their effects. Every passenger who arrives at the ports of the Republic, can disembark at once after the vessel has cast anchor. together with his personal baggage. In case the vessel should arrive at night, or at any hour that the office of the custom-house is closed, passengers will be allowed to disembark, but will only be allowed to take with them a small object or box containing not more than may be necessary for immediate personal wants.

The examination of baggage will be made liberally, with prudence and moderation. Passengers will not be detained any longer than the time necessary for inspection of the objects which are in their possession, and should they be foreigners not speaking or understanding the Spanish language, there will be at the examination an employé who will serve as interpreter, whose duty it will be to inform passengers of the conditions and formalities to which they are obliged to submit, in conformity with customs, tariff and other dispositions relative thereto. In regard to wearing apparel and jewelry of personal use, it will be left subject to the examination of the officers as to the quantity and quality of that which will not be subject to duty, taking into consideration the character and personality of the travelers.

The articles which ought to be considered commonly used, besides the wearing apparel, and which are dispatched free of duty, are the following, observing, however, that duty will be collected on such objects which may be found between said articles presented by the travelers which cannot, in a *bona fide* sense, be materially used by them.

Two watches with their chains.

100 cigars.

40 small boxes of cigarettes.

½ kilog. of snuff.

½ kilog. smoking tobacco.

One pair of pistols with accessory and with 200 charges.

A rifle, a gun or fowling piece, with accessory and with 200 charges.

One pair of musical instruments, excepting piano-fortes or organs.

All those objects not included into the franchise granted into the preceding lines, and which are carried by the travelers in small quantities with the motive of making presents, are subject to the duties fixed in the tariff.

They are obliged to make respecting them a declaration explaining the number of the packages and their contents, handing it over to the Custom House.

When there arrives with the effects of travelers used furniture, it will be taken into account their demerit for the settlement of the duties.

Should the travelers be artists of some opera, drama, opera company, etc., it will be allowed in general to them, besides the franchise granted in the preceding article, the introduction free from duty of their costumes, scenic ornaments, but so that the same will arrive forming a portion of their effects and are not of an excessive quantity. Should the officers be of opinion that there is some abuse with the introduction, they have to make up an invoice and to collect 55% on the valuation or appraisement which is to be done in the same form as with those effects which ought to pay on appraisement.

Loose sheets containing these particulars have been printed by order of the Custom House and are distributed by the purser of the vessel among passengers before the dispatch of their effects. These forms are printed in Spanish, French, English and German, in order that passengers may acquaint themselves with the obligations to which they are subject.

LINES OF STEAMERS ARRIVING AT VERA CRUZ.

TIME TABLE AND PASSENGER RATES.

ROYAL MAIL LINE.

Steamer arrives at Vera Cruz on the 27th or 28th of every month; leaves Vera Cruz for Havana and Southampton on the first and second of every month.

Passage rates to Southampton, first class,	.	$236.43	$210.18	$183.97
" " " second class,	.	121.37		
" " " third class,	.	78.81		

Agents in Vera Cruz, Cos, Castillo & Co.

FRENCH TRANSATLANTIC LINE.

Steamer arrives at Vera Cruz on the 13th to 15th of every month; leaves Vera Cruz for Havana and St. Nazaire on the 17th of every month.

| Passage rates to St. Nazaire, first class, | . | $280.00 | $252.00 | $190.00 |
| " " " steerage, | . | 114.00 | | |

Agents in Vera Cruz, Torre, Fisher & Co.

GERMAN LINE.

Steamer arrives at Vera Cruz on the 6th of every month; leaves Vera Cruz for Tampico on the 7th, and returns to Vera Cruz; leaves Vera Cruz for Havana and Hamburg on the 12th.

Passage rates to Hamburg, first class,
"   "   "   steerage,   .
Agents in Vera Cruz, GUILLERMO BUSING & Co.

LIVERPOOL LINE.

Steamer arrives at Vera Cruz on the 6th to 10th of every month; leaves Vera Cruz for New Orleans *via* Tampico and Brazos on the 25th to 30th of every month.

Passage rates to New Orleans, 1st class, $60.00
"   "   "   2d class.   .   .   .   45.00
Agents in Vera Cruz, M. Z. DE MARKOE & Co.

AMERICAN LINE FROM NEW YORK.

Steamer leaves New York for Vera Cruz during the summer months every two weeks, touching at the ports of Havana, Progreso, Campeche and Frontera; during the winter months steamer leaves every week, touching at the same ports, going and coming.

Passage rates from New York to Vera Cruz,   .   . $85.00
"   "   .   ..   "   and return,   .   .   .   100.00
Agents in Vera Cruz, R. C. RITTER & Co.

AMERICAN LINE FROM NEW ORLEANS.

Steamers leave New Orleans for Vera Cruz every three weeks, touching at the ports of Bagdad, Tampico and Tuxpam, going and coming.

PASSENGER RATES FROM VERA CRUZ TO

	Havana.	New York.	New Orleans.
American steamer, 1st class. .	$50.00	$85.00	$60.00
" " 2d class,	25.00	60.00	45.00
English steamer, 1st class,	52.56		
" " 2d class, .	26.31		
French steamer, 1st class,	52.00		
" " 2d class, . .	26.00		
German steamer, 1st class,	59.00		
" " steerage, .	15.00		
Liverpool steamer, 1st class.			60.00
" " 2d class,			45.00

RAILROAD TIME TABLE AND PASSAGE RATES
FROM VERA·CRUZ TO MEXICO.

STATIONS.			1st Class.	2d Class.	3d Class.
Vera Cruz	Leave	11 30 P.M.			
Tejeria	"	12 05 A.M.	$ 0 71	$ 0 52	$ 0 28
Soleda	Arrive	1 ı 0	1 92	1 40	0 75
"	Leave	1 10	—	—	—
Camaron	"	2 05	2 8ı	1 10	1 13
Paso del Macho	Arrive	2 35	3 47	2 53	1 36
" "	Leave	2 55	—	—	—
Atoyac	"	3 25	3 93	2 86	1 53
Cordoba	Arrive	4 20	4 83	3 52	1 89
"	Leave	1 30	—	—	—
Fortin	"	5 00	6 20	3 78	2 03
Orizaba	Arrive	6 00	7 03	4 39	2 35
"	Leave	6 20	—	—	—
Encinal			—	—	—
Maltrata	Leave	7 20	7 96	5 06	2 72
Bota	"	8 05	—	—	—
Alta Luz			—	—	—
Boca del Monte			7 88	5 73	3 08
Esperanza	Arrive	9 20	—	—	—
"	Leave	10 00	—	—	—
San Andres	"	10 50	8 87	6 56	3 59
Rinconada	"	11 20	9 54	7 11	3 92
San Marcos	Arrive	11 40	10 12	7 50	4 23
"	Leave	11 50	—	—	—
Huamantla	"	12 35 P. M.	10 68	8 06	5 51
Apizaco	Arrive	1 25	11 50	8 75	4 94
"	Leave	1 55	—	—	—
Guadalupe (hacienda)	"	2 35	11 99	9 16	5 19
Soltepec	"	3 05	12 37	9 48	5 39
Apam	Arrive	3 35	13 00	10 00	5 71
"	Leave	3 45	—	—	—
Trolo	"	4 15	13 50	10 42	5 97
Ometusco	"	4 40	13 82	10 58	6 13
La Palma	"	4 55	14 02	10 85	6 23
Otumba	"	5 18	14 21	11 01	6 33
S. Juan Teotihuacan	"	5 40	14 59	11 32	6 52
Texpam	"	5 55	14 95	11 62	6 71
Mexico	Arrive	6 50	16 00	12 50	7 25

BRANCH LINE FROM PUEBLA TO APIZACO.

Train to Mexico.	Train to Veracruz.	Distance in Miles.	Distance in Kilometres	STATIONS.	1st Class.	2d Class.	3d Class.
Morning 11 00	Night. 12 00			Puebla			
11 30	12 30	7½	12	Pauzacola	$0 59	$0 4	$0 30
12 15	1 15	18¾	30¼	Santa Ana	0 93	0 78	0 58
1 00	2 00	29¼	47	Apizaco	1 52	1 27	0 78

BRANCH LINE FBOM VERA CRUZ TO JALAPA.

STATIONS.	1st Class.	2d Class.
Veracruz..		
Tejeria..	$0 87	$0 56
Paso de San Juan	1 50	0 93
Tierra Colorado	1 87	1 12
Paso de Olivas	2 62	1 62
Puente Nacional	3 25	2 00
Ruiconada	3 75	2 31
Plan del Rio	4 05	2 65
Cerro Gordo	5 12	3 12
Dos Rios	5 75	3 50
Jalapa	6 50	4 00

EXCURSIONS FROM HAVANA.

1. Havana to Batabano by rail; thence by steamer to Cienfuegos, Trinidad, Manzanillo, Santiago de Cuba, Baracoa, Gibara, Nuevitas, Havana— or in reverse order.

2. Havana to Santiago de Cuba, as in No. 1; thence by steamer to Kingston, Jamaica, and return to Santiago.

3. Havana steamer to Nuevitas, Santiago, Porto Plata, Porto Rico, St. Thomas (Spanish line).

4. Havana to St. Thomas by Royal Mail and French Line of Steamers direct.

5. Havana to St. Thomas, as in No. 4; thence to Antigua, Barbados, Dominica, Granada, Guadalcupe, Martinique, St. Lucia, St. Vincent and other islands; returning same way.

6. Steamer to St. Thomas; thence to Para, Bahia, Pernambuco, Rio de Janairo, by Brazil Line American steamers.

7. Steamer to St. Thomas; thence to New York by Brazil Line American steamers.

8. Steamer to St. Thomas; thence to England or France by Royal Mail or French steamers.

9. Havana to Vera Cruz and other Mexican ports, by Alexandre's Line.

10. Havana to Cedar Keys and New Orleans; connecting at Cedar Keys with railroad to Florida cities and the North.

11. Havana to New Orleans direct, and rail to all points in the United States and Canada.

12. Havana to Nassau; thence to St. Augustine and Savannah, Ga.

13. Havana to Matanzas, Cardenas, Sagua, Cienfuegos, by railroad (various routes).

14. Havana to tobacco districts, by Western Railroad.

15. Havana to tobacco district of Vuelta Abajo, by steamer to Bahia Honda and San Cayetano.

STEAMSHIP LINES FROM HAVANA.

SPANISH MAIL LINE.

For Coruna and Santader, Spain, on the 15th, monthly.
For Cadiz, 5th and 25th, monthly.

First Class, ...	$200 00
Second Class, -	160 00
Third Class, ...	70 00

Agents, M. Calvo & Co.,
No. 28 Oficios street.

WEST INDIA MAIL STEAMSHIP LINE.

Leave Havana on the 3d, 10th, 13th and 23d, monthly, for Santiago de

Cuba, Puerto Rico, St. Thomas, Kingston, touching at principal Cuban and
Puerto Rico ports.

	1st class.	2d class.
Havana to Nuevitas,	$34 00	$23 00
" " Gibara,	41 00	28 00
" " Santiago,	51 00	34 00
" " Kingston, .	. . . . .	. . . . .
" " Puerto Plata,	60 00	40 00
" " Puerto Rico,	65 00	40 00
" " St. Thomas, . . .	65 00	40 00

Agent, DN RAMON DE HERRERA,
No. 68 Oficios Street.

MISSISSIPPI AND DOMINION STEAMSHIP LINE.

HAVANA TO NEW ORLEANS AND LIVERPOOL.

Monthly trips between each port.

	1st class.	2d class.
Havana to New Orleans,	$34 00	$17 00
" " Liverpool, . . .	140 00	40 00

Agents, J. H. DURRUTY & Co.,
No. 23 San Ignacio Street.

NORDDEUTSCHER LLOYD STEAMSHIP CO.

BREMEN AND NEW ORLEANS, TOUCHING AT SOUTHAMPTON AND HAVRE.

Leaving Havana every 15 days during the winter.

	1st class.	2d class.
Havana to New Orleans, ...	$34 00	17 00
" " Europe, ...	153 00	51 00

Agents, H. UPMANN & Co.,
64 Cuba Street.

NEW ORLEANS, FLORIDA AND HAVANA STEAMSHIP COMPANY.

HAVANA TO NEW ORLEANS, TOUCHING AT KEY WEST AND CEDAR KEYS, FLORIDA.

Leave Havana every Wednesday.

Havana to Key West,	. . . . . .	$10 00
" " Cedar Keys, .	. . .	25 00
" " New Orleans	. . . . . .	34 00

Agents, LAWTON BROTHERS,
No. 13 Mercaderes Street.

SOUTH SIDE COAST LINE.

HAVANA TO ISLE OF PINES.

Via Railroad to Batabano, Cuba. Leave Havana by rail every Sunday morning.

	1st class.	2d class.
Batabano to Nueva Gerona, . . .	$9 00	$5 50

NOTE.—The Island of Pines is a noted place for invalids, and strongly recommended by medical men.

SOUTHERN NAVIGATION LINE.

HAVANA TO CIENFUEGOS, TRINIDAD AND SANTIAGO DE CUBA, VIA RAILROAD TO BATABANO.

Leave Havana (Central Railroad) every Sunday at 2.40 P. M., and every Wednesday at 5.45 A. M., for Batabano, connecting with first-class steamers.

Batabano to Cienfuegos	. . . . .	$
" " Trinidad,	. . . . .	
" " Manzanillo	. . . . .	
" " Santiago de Cuba,	.	

HAVANA TO CARDENAS.

Spanish steamer "Soler" every Tuesday and Friday, at 6 P. M. Returns every Wednesday and Saturday.

First-class passage, ... $10 0

HAVANA TO CAIBARIEN.

Touching at Cardenas every 10th, 20th and 30th of the month, per steamship "Alava."

Havana to Nuevitas, Gibara, Baracoa, Guantanamo and Santiago, Spanish steamer "Clara," every 15 days.

Agents, L. SOHLER & Co.,
No. 10 Paula Street.

HAVANA TO SAGUA AND CAIBARIEN, TOUCHING AT CARDENAS.

SPANISH STEAMER "DOMINGO N. HERNANDER."

Leave Havana 5th, 15th and 25th, monthly.

	1st class.	2d class.
Havana to Sagua, ...	$25 00	$15 00
" " Caibarien, . .	40 00	20 00
Sagua to Caibarien, ...	16 00	8 00
Above in Spanish bank-bills.		

HAVANA TO BAHIA HONDA, SAN-CAYETANO, RIO BLANCO, &c. (TOBACCO DISTRICT).

STEAMERS "BAHIA HONDA" AND "ANITA".

Every Saturday at 10 P. M.

	1st class.	2d class.
Havana to Bahia Honda, . .	$6 37	$ 5 00
" " Rio Blanco, .	10 62	8 50
" " San Cayetano, .	12 75	10 62
" Malas Aguas, ...	14 87	12 75

VANA TO NASSAU, N. P.; THENCE TO ST. ATGUSTINE, FLA.,
AND SAVANNAH, GA.

Leave every fortnight.
All rates not otherwise specified are in Spanish gold.

S. S. CITY OF ALEXANDRIA.

Was built by John Roach & Sons, Chester, Pa., on July 9th, 1880; she is
338 feet long over all, 38 feet 6 inches wide, 25 feet deep from the spar deck,
and 33 feet deep from the hurricane deck, being 10 feet longer, 6 inches
wider and 2 feet shallower than the "City of Washington, which in all other
respects she closely resembles. The hull is iron with plates from five eighths
of an inch to one inch in thickness, which are riveted in boiler style; the
deck houses around the galley and the boiler and engine rooms are also iron,
but in other places of wood; the spar deck for the entire length and breadth
of the vessel is of iron covered with wood, and the lower deck abreast of the
machinery is of iron. The engines are a compound pair with a high pressure
cylinder of 42½ inches and a low pressure cylinder of 78 inches diameter and
with a stroke of 54 inches. Steam is furnished at 80 pounds per square inch
by four boilers, each 10 feet long by 14 feet 6 inches in diameter and each
having four furnaces. The total grate surface is 352 feet. The propeller is of
the Hirsch pattern, 16 feet 3 inches in diameter with a pitch of 25 feet; the
vessel has a water ballast tank and a fresh water condenser, capable of producing 250 gallons per day, and she carries as a part of her general equipment,
which is thorough in every department, a steam launch.

The steamer has superb accommodations for 150 first class passengers :
the large saloon, is in the section where the least motion is felt and
where the greatest amount of light and breeze are attainable at sea ; it is
fitted with small tables whereat passengers may breakfast, dine or sup *a la
carte* and at any hour; each table is made to accomodate four persons and is
supplied with revolving chairs. The joiner work is a marvel of beauty and
taste, the main saloon is furnished in ash, mahogany, black walnut, butternut
white holly, and amaranth, or as it is called in South America "blood woot,'
all highly polished and arranged in an exqnisitely artistic manner. There are

five spacious bridal chambers. The berths are constructed in cane bottoms for use in warm weather and swinging berths are in readiness for sea sick passengers; each room is neatly furnished and supplied with every convenience to make the occupants comfortable. In the matter of life preservers and life boats the City of Alexandria cannot be surpassed by any other steamship afloat; she is commanded by Captain J. Deaken, commodore of Alexandre's Line, an old and experienced navigator; who was captain of the first steamer that Messrs. Alexandre sent to Mexico and has since successfully commanded every new steamer this company has had. Those who have traveled with the commodore are universal in their high praises of him as a gentleman and officer.

S. S. CITY OF WASHINGTON.

Is an iron steamer built by Messrs. John Roach & Sons, of Chester, Pa. The vessel is 2618 tons custom house measurement. Its dimensions are 321 feet; breadth of beam, 38 feet; depth from spar deck, 35 feet; and from hurricane deck, 28 feet. Her hull is of iron, the plating being riveted throughout in boiler fashion, the plates vary from five-eighths of an inch to an inch and a quarter in thickness; her deck houses near the machinery and the galley are of iron, while the others are constructed of wood; the spar deck is of iron covered with wood for the entire length and breadth of the vessel; the lower deck abreast of the space occupied by the machinery is also of iron. The engines were made at the Morgan Iron Works of New York, they are of the compound pattern, the high pressure cylinder having a diameter of 40 inches and the low pressure one of 74 inches; the stroke of the piston is six feet. The boilers, two in number, have each a diameter of 17 feet and a height of 20 feet, the steam pressure is 80 lbs to the square inch; the propeller has a diameter of 16 feet with a pitch of 24 feet. The City of Washington can accommodate 150 first-class passengers. The state rooms are fitted up finely employing all the resources of artistic joiners; the saloon is made from 20 different kinds of wood from black walnut to amaranth; the latter wood is somewhat like red cedar but has a finer grain, a more beautiful color and is susceptible of a more perfect polish. With a view of preventing sea sickness and greatly adding to the comfort of passengers there has been placed in a number of state rooms the new patent " Huston " self-leveling berth which remains always and under all circumstances in a perfectly horizontal position however great may be the rolling and pitching of the steamer, this can not fail to be appreciated by the travelers and especially those effected by sea sickness who may now feel assured of enjoying perfect rest and quiet while in their berths. A change has also been introduced in the dining saloons, where, instead of the inconvenient long tables and sofas of the old style, small tables that will accommodate from four to eight persons have been substituted, with single revolving chairs for each one in order to avoid the usual confusion and noise incident to the dining together of all the passengers. L. F. Timmermann is Captain.

S. S. CITY OF MEXICO.

Was built by Messrs. John Englis & Son of New York, and is 219 feet in length on deck, 36 feet beam, 20 feet depth of hold and 1027 tons burthen. She is constructed of white oak, hackmatack and chestnut, and fastened with composition and galvanized iron; her engines, constructed by the Quintard Iron Works, are of the vertical direct acting character, 50 inches diameter of cylinder by 44 inches stroke, her propeller, 13 feet diameter, has a pitch of 25 feet. She is fitted with auxiliary boilers and steam pumps of the largest capacity; her internal fittings reflect credit on both joiners and upholsterers as the 49 state rooms and 101 berths she possesses, are furnished in the most comfortable manner with all that a veteran *voyageur* could desire. All the necessary hoisting engines, steam pumps, auxiliary boilers, &c., that a vessel of this character requires, the City of Mexico has in abundance.—J. McIntosh is the Commander.

S. S. CITY OF MERIDA.

Was built by Messrs. John Englis & Son of Greenpoint, L. I.; she is 265 feet in length on deck, 37 feet beam, 26½ feet in depth of hold (in lower hold 11 feet in depth) height between decks 8 feet, in Cabin 7½ feet; she is 2000 tons old or 1500 tons custom house measurement, full brig rigged, has surface condenser engines (built at the Delamater works) of 56 inch cylinder, 54 inch cylinder, 54 inch stroke of piston, with two return tubular boilers: she has two smoke stacks and a brass screw, weighing 2000 pounds. Her state rooms of which there are forty first-class and twelve second-class are fitted magnificently, and their arrangement and adornment are simply superb. A peculiarity of the interior arrangements is that the deck appartments are fitted with steam radiators and communication by wire and bell between the stewards department and every state room is ingeniously provided for. The appearance of the ship is such that even the most ignorant landsman must have confidence in her. She is high in the bows and has a clear run aft, and altogether may be described as a safe and swift vessel in which it would be a comfort to travel. J. W. Reynolds is Captain.

S. S. BRITISH EMPIRE.

This steamer is chartered by Messrs. F. Alexandre & Sons. It is an iron steamer and was built in 1878 for New Zealand trade ; it is 410 feet long, 40 feet beam, 28 feet hold, and has a carrying capacity of 4000 tons. She is supplied with two 3000 horse power compound engines; she was constructed and built by the same firm, who build the steamers of the white star line. The steamer being too large for the trade in which it was engaged, it was placed on the line between Liverpool and Philadelphia, from whom it is chartered; it has superior accommodations for 50 first-class passengers and 40 second-class. The dining rooms are on deck midship of the steamer, and the state rooms are furnished with all modern improvements and she is considered as safe and comfortable a steamer as any on the line. Captain Fawcett is commander with Captain Rettig as first officer.

S. S. NANKIN.

Is an iron built screw steamer of 3100 tons capacity, chartered by Messrs. F. Alexandre & Sons, and is in every respect adapted for the trade in which it is engaged. As for comfort it cannot be surpassed by any steamer afloat. Her length is 331 feet, breadth 36 feet 8 inches, depth of hold 25 feet 7 inches. The cabins and dining rooms are amidships, the smoking room and social hall are on the upper deck, and every room is supplied with every convenience to make the occupants comfortable. In the matter of life preservers the steamship Nankin is supplied in abundance.

Henry Prouse Cooper
Tailor and Importer
292 Fifth Avenue,
and 54 Broadway,
New York.

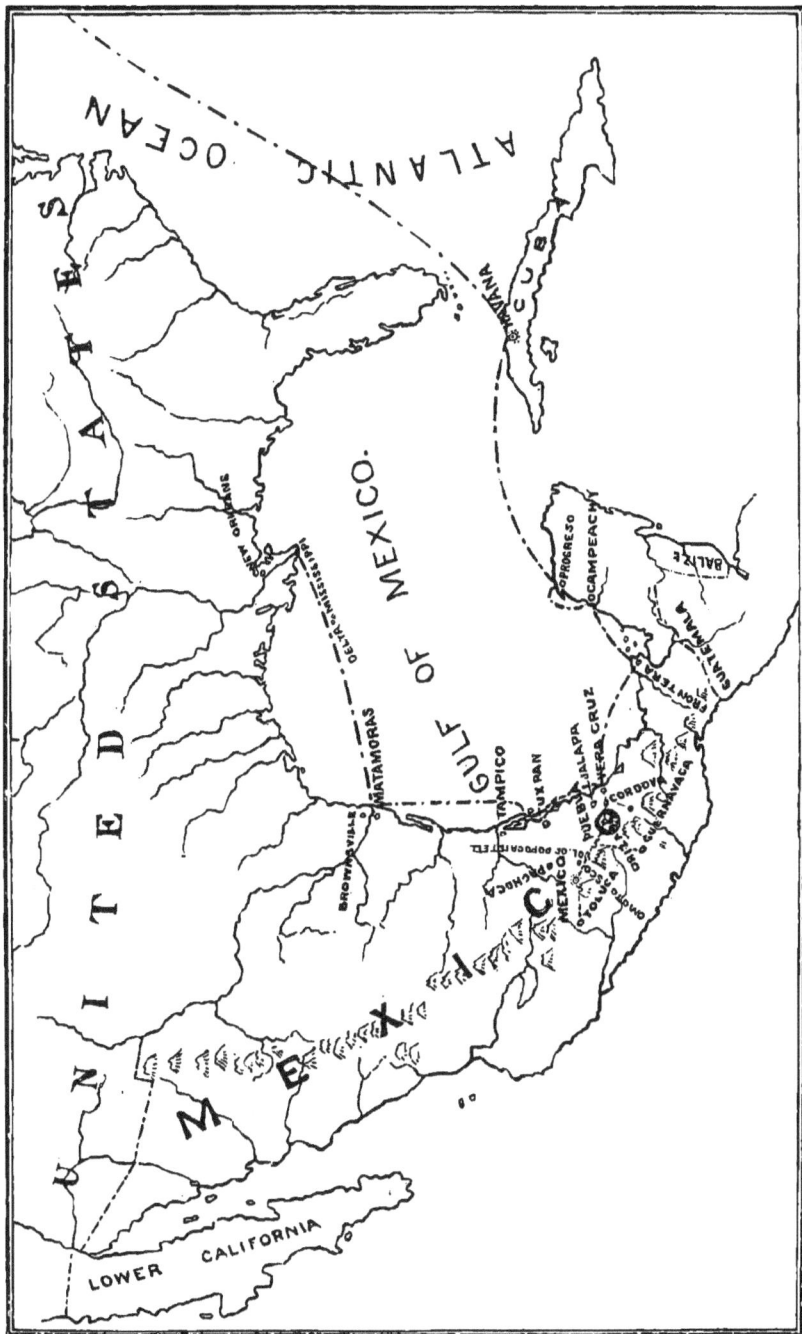

STEAMSHIP ROUTE OF F. ALEXANDRE & SONS TO HAVANA AND MEXICO.

www.ingramcontent.com/pod-product-compliance
Lightning Source LLC
Chambersburg PA
CBHW020238090426
42735CB00010B/1745